The Glorious Mysteries

AN ILLUSTRATED ROSARY BOOK FOR KIDS AND THEIR FAMILIES

THE ILLUMINATED ROSARY
Revised Edition

TEXT BY JERRY WINDLEY-DAOUST
ORIGINAL CONCEPT BY MARK DAOUST

For an introduction to praying the rosary with this book, see page 92.

The Canticle of Mary (Magnificat)

My soul proclaims the greatness of the Lord;
   my spirit rejoices in God my Savior
   for he has looked with favor on his lowly servant.
From this day all generations will call me blessed;
   the Almighty has done great things for me
   and holy is his name.
He has mercy on those who fear him
   in every generation.
He has shown the strength of his arm,
   and has scattered the proud in their conceit.
He has cast down the mighty from their thrones,
   and has lifted up the lowly.
He has filled the hungry with good things,
   and the rich he has sent away empty.
He has come to the help of his servant Israel
   for he has remembered his promise of mercy,
   the promise he made to our fathers,
   to Abraham and his children forever.

In the name of the Father,
   and of the Son, and of the Holy Spirit.
Amen.

I believe
   in God, the Father almighty,
   Creator of heaven and earth,
and in Jesus Christ,
   his only Son, our Lord,
   who was conceived by the Holy Spirit,
born of the Virgin Mary,
   suffered under Pontius Pilate,
was crucified, died and was buried;
he descended into hell;
   on the third day he rose again from the dead;
he ascended into heaven,
   and is seated at the right hand
   of God the Father almighty;
from there he will come to judge
   the living and the dead.

I believe in the Holy Spirit,
   the holy catholic Church,
   the communion of saints,
   the forgiveness of sins,
   the resurrection of the body,
   and life everlasting.
Amen.

Our Father
  who art in heaven,
   hallowed be thy name.
Thy kingdom come.
Thy will be done on earth,
   as it is in heaven.

Give us this day our daily bread,
and forgive us our trespasses,
as we forgive those
   who trespass against us,
and lead us not into temptation,
   but deliver us from evil.

Amen.

FOR FAITH

Hail, Mary, full of grace, the Lord is with thee.
Blessed art thou among women,
and blessed is the fruit of thy womb, Jesus.
Holy Mary, Mother of God, pray for us sinners,
now and at the hour of our death. *Amen.*

FOR HOPE

Hail, Mary, full of grace, the Lord is with thee.
Blessed art thou among women,
and blessed is the fruit of thy womb, Jesus.
Holy Mary, Mother of God, pray for us sinners,
now and at the hour of our death. *Amen.*

FOR CHARITY

Hail, Mary, full of grace, the Lord is with thee.
Blessed art thou among women,
and blessed is the fruit of thy womb, Jesus.
Holy Mary, Mother of God, pray for us sinners,
now and at the hour of our death. *Amen.*

Glory be to the Father,
and to the Son, and to the Holy Spirit;
as it was in the beginning, is now, and ever shall be
world without end. *Amen.*

The Resurrection

At dawn on the first day of the week,
Mary Magdalene and some other women
took spices to the tomb of Jesus;
but when they arrived,
the tomb was empty.

An angel appeared to them, saying,
"Do not be afraid! You are seeking
Jesus the crucified. He is not here,
for he has been raised just as he said."

The women ran away from the tomb,
fearful but overjoyed,
and told the disciples everything.
But they did not believe the story
until Jesus appeared in their midst,
saying, "Peace be with you!
Why do questions arise in your hearts?
Touch me and see that it is I myself."

INTENTIONS

Our Father
   who art in heaven,
   hallowed be thy name.
Thy kingdom come.
Thy will be done on earth,
   as it is in heaven.

Give us this day our daily bread,
and forgive us our trespasses,
as we forgive those
   who trespass against us,
and lead us not into temptation,
   but deliver us from evil.

Amen.

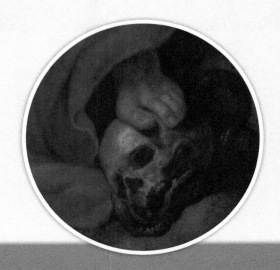

Hail, Mary, full of grace, the Lord is with thee.
Blessed art thou among women,
and blessed is the fruit of thy womb, Jesus.

Holy Mary, Mother of God, pray for us sinners,
now and at the hour of our death. *Amen.*

Hail, Mary, full of grace, the Lord is with thee.
Blessed art thou among women,
and blessed is the fruit of thy womb, Jesus.

Holy Mary, Mother of God, pray for us sinners,
now and at the hour of our death. *Amen.*

The Resurrection

Hail, Mary, full of grace, the Lord is with thee.
Blessed art thou among women,
and blessed is the fruit of thy womb, Jesus.

Holy Mary, Mother of God, pray for us sinners,
now and at the hour of our death. *Amen.*

Hail, Mary, full of grace, the Lord is with thee.
Blessed art thou among women,
and blessed is the fruit of thy womb, Jesus.

Holy Mary, Mother of God, pray for us sinners,
now and at the hour of our death. *Amen.*

Hail, Mary, full of grace, the Lord is with thee.
Blessed art thou among women,
and blessed is the fruit of thy womb, Jesus.

Holy Mary, Mother of God, pray for us sinners,
now and at the hour of our death. *Amen.*

Hail, Mary, full of grace, the Lord is with thee.
Blessed art thou among women,
and blessed is the fruit of thy womb, Jesus.

Holy Mary, Mother of God, pray for us sinners,
now and at the hour of our death. *Amen.*

Hail, Mary, full of grace, the Lord is with thee.
Blessed art thou among women,
and blessed is the fruit of thy womb, Jesus.

Holy Mary, Mother of God, pray for us sinners,
now and at the hour of our death. *Amen.*

Hail, Mary, full of grace, the Lord is with thee.
Blessed art thou among women,
and blessed is the fruit of thy womb, Jesus.

Holy Mary, Mother of God, pray for us sinners,
now and at the hour of our death. *Amen.*

Hail, Mary, full of grace, the Lord is with thee.
Blessed art thou among women,
and blessed is the fruit of thy womb, Jesus.

Holy Mary, Mother of God, pray for us sinners,
now and at the hour of our death. *Amen.*

Hail, Mary, full of grace, the Lord is with thee.
  Blessed art thou among women,
    and blessed is the fruit of thy womb, Jesus.

Holy Mary, Mother of God, pray for us sinners,
  now and at the hour of our death. *Amen.*

Glory be to the Father,
  and to the Son, and to the Holy Spirit;
as it was in the beginning, is now,
and ever shall be, world without end.
  Amen.

O my Jesus, forgive us our sins,
save us from the fires of hell;
lead all souls to heaven, especially
those in most need of thy mercy.

The Ascension

Jesus said to the disciples,
"All power in heaven and on earth
has been given to me. Go, therefore,
and make disciples of all nations,
baptizing them in the name of the Father,
and of the Son,
and of the Holy Spirit,
teaching them to observe
all that I have commanded you.
And behold, I am with you always."

Then Jesus led them out to Bethany,
raised his hands, and blessed them.
As he blessed them he parted from them
and was taken up to heaven.
They worshipped him
and then returned to Jerusalem
with great joy.

INTENTIONS

Our Father
　who art in heaven,
　hallowed be thy name.
Thy kingdom come.
Thy will be done on earth,
　as it is in heaven.

Give us this day our daily bread,
and forgive us our trespasses,
as we forgive those
　who trespass against us,
and lead us not into temptation,
　but deliver us from evil.

Amen.

The Ascension

Hail, Mary, full of grace, the Lord is with thee.
Blessed art thou among women,
and blessed is the fruit of thy womb, Jesus.

Holy Mary, Mother of God, pray for us sinners,
now and at the hour of our death. *Amen.*

Hail, Mary, full of grace, the Lord is with thee.
  Blessed art thou among women,
    and blessed is the fruit of thy womb, Jesus.

Holy Mary, Mother of God, pray for us sinners,
  now and at the hour of our death. *Amen.*

Hail, Mary, full of grace, the Lord is with thee.
Blessed art thou among women,
and blessed is the fruit of thy womb, Jesus.

Holy Mary, Mother of God, pray for us sinners,
now and at the hour of our death. *Amen.*

Hail, Mary, full of grace, the Lord is with thee.
Blessed art thou among women,
and blessed is the fruit of thy womb, Jesus.

Holy Mary, Mother of God, pray for us sinners,
now and at the hour of our death. *Amen.*

Hail, Mary, full of grace, the Lord is with thee.
Blessed art thou among women,
and blessed is the fruit of thy womb, Jesus.

Holy Mary, Mother of God, pray for us sinners,
now and at the hour of our death. *Amen.*

Hail, Mary, full of grace, the Lord is with thee.
Blessed art thou among women,
and blessed is the fruit of thy womb, Jesus.

Holy Mary, Mother of God, pray for us sinners,
now and at the hour of our death. *Amen.*

Hail, Mary, full of grace, the Lord is with thee.
Blessed art thou among women,
and blessed is the fruit of thy womb, Jesus.

Holy Mary, Mother of God, pray for us sinners,
now and at the hour of our death. *Amen.*

Hail, Mary, full of grace, the Lord is with thee.
Blessed art thou among women,
and blessed is the fruit of thy womb, Jesus.

Holy Mary, Mother of God, pray for us sinners,
now and at the hour of our death. *Amen.*

Hail, Mary, full of grace, the Lord is with thee.
Blessed art thou among women,
and blessed is the fruit of thy womb, Jesus.

Holy Mary, Mother of God, pray for us sinners,
now and at the hour of our death. *Amen.*

Hail, Mary, full of grace, the Lord is with thee.
 Blessed art thou among women,
  and blessed is the fruit of thy womb, Jesus.

Holy Mary, Mother of God, pray for us sinners,
 now and at the hour of our death. *Amen.*

Glory be to the Father,
 and to the Son, and to the Holy Spirit;
as it was in the beginning, is now,
and ever shall be, world without end.
 Amen.

O my Jesus, forgive us our sins,
save us from the fires of hell;
lead all souls to heaven, especially
those in most need of thy mercy.

The Descent of the Holy Spirit

On the feast of Pentecost,
Jesus' friends were gathered
with Mary, the mother of Jesus,
when suddenly a noise
like a strong driving wind
came from the sky,
filling the entire house;
and tongues as of fire
came to rest on each one of them.
and they were all filled
with the Holy Spirit,
who enabled them to proclaim
the Gospel in the language
of every nation under heaven.

INTENTIONS

Our Father

who art in heaven,
hallowed be thy name.
Thy kingdom come.
Thy will be done on earth,
as it is in heaven.

Give us this day our daily bread,
and forgive us our trespasses,
as we forgive those
who trespass against us,
and lead us not into temptation,
but deliver us from evil.

Amen.

Hail, Mary, full of grace, the Lord is with thee.
Blessed art thou among women,
and blessed is the fruit of thy womb, Jesus.

Holy Mary, Mother of God, pray for us sinners,
now and at the hour of our death. *Amen.*

Hail, Mary, full of grace, the Lord is with thee.
Blessed art thou among women,
and blessed is the fruit of thy womb, Jesus.

Holy Mary, Mother of God, pray for us sinners,
now and at the hour of our death. *Amen.*

Hail, Mary, full of grace, the Lord is with thee.
Blessed art thou among women,
and blessed is the fruit of thy womb, Jesus.

Holy Mary, Mother of God, pray for us sinners,
now and at the hour of our death. *Amen.*

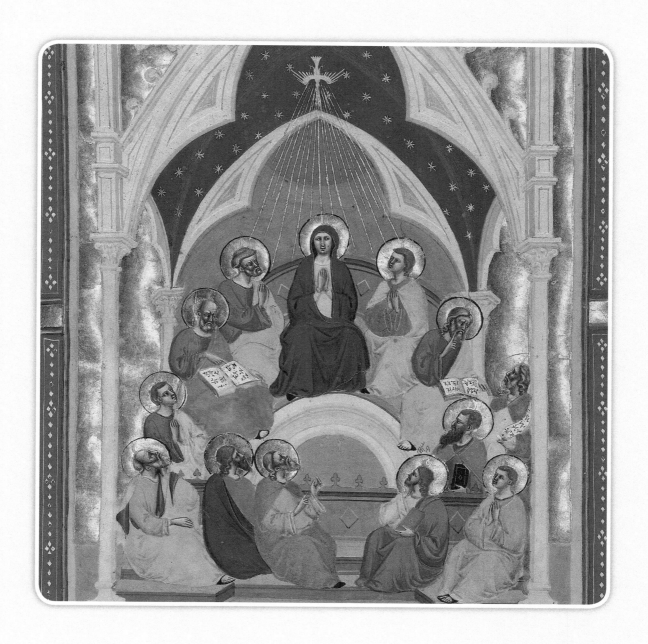

Hail, Mary, full of grace, the Lord is with thee.
  Blessed art thou among women,
    and blessed is the fruit of thy womb, Jesus.

Holy Mary, Mother of God, pray for us sinners,
  now and at the hour of our death. *Amen.*

Hail, Mary, full of grace, the Lord is with thee.
Blessed art thou among women,
and blessed is the fruit of thy womb, Jesus.

Holy Mary, Mother of God, pray for us sinners,
now and at the hour of our death. *Amen.*

Hail, Mary, full of grace, the Lord is with thee.
Blessed art thou among women,
and blessed is the fruit of thy womb, Jesus.

Holy Mary, Mother of God, pray for us sinners,
now and at the hour of our death. *Amen.*

Hail, Mary, full of grace, the Lord is with thee.
Blessed art thou among women,
and blessed is the fruit of thy womb, Jesus.

Holy Mary, Mother of God, pray for us sinners,
now and at the hour of our death. *Amen.*

Hail, Mary, full of grace, the Lord is with thee.
Blessed art thou among women,
    and blessed is the fruit of thy womb, Jesus.

Holy Mary, Mother of God, pray for us sinners,
    now and at the hour of our death.   *Amen.*

Hail, Mary, full of grace, the Lord is with thee.
Blessed art thou among women,
and blessed is the fruit of thy womb, Jesus.

Holy Mary, Mother of God, pray for us sinners,
now and at the hour of our death. *Amen.*

Hail, Mary, full of grace, the Lord is with thee.
Blessed art thou among women,
and blessed is the fruit of thy womb, Jesus.

Holy Mary, Mother of God, pray for us sinners,
now and at the hour of our death. *Amen.*

Glory be to the Father,
   and to the Son, and to the Holy Spirit;
as it was in the beginning, is now,
and ever shall be, world without end.
   Amen.

O my Jesus, forgive us our sins,
save us from the fires of hell;
lead all souls to heaven, especially
those in most need of thy mercy.

The Assumption

When the apostles heard
that Mary, the mother of Jesus,
was going to be taken from this world,
they gathered at her house
and kept watch with her.

And behold, the Lord Jesus
did not let the one
in whose womb he had dwelled
see the corruption of death;
but instead, he came with his angels
and took her up to heaven
as the beginning and image
of the Church coming to perfection,
and a sign of sure hope
and comfort to God's people.

INTENTIONS

Our Father
 who art in heaven,
  hallowed be thy name.
Thy kingdom come.
Thy will be done on earth,
  as it is in heaven.

Give us this day our daily bread,
and forgive us our trespasses,
as we forgive those
  who trespass against us,
and lead us not into temptation,
  but deliver us from evil.

Amen.

Hail, Mary, full of grace, the Lord is with thee.
Blessed art thou among women,
and blessed is the fruit of thy womb, Jesus.

Holy Mary, Mother of God, pray for us sinners,
now and at the hour of our death. *Amen.*

Hail, Mary, full of grace, the Lord is with thee.
Blessed art thou among women,
and blessed is the fruit of thy womb, Jesus.

Holy Mary, Mother of God, pray for us sinners,
now and at the hour of our death. *Amen.*

Hail, Mary, full of grace, the Lord is with thee.
Blessed art thou among women,
and blessed is the fruit of thy womb, Jesus.

Holy Mary, Mother of God, pray for us sinners,
now and at the hour of our death. *Amen.*

Hail, Mary, full of grace, the Lord is with thee.
Blessed art thou among women,
and blessed is the fruit of thy womb, Jesus.

Holy Mary, Mother of God, pray for us sinners,
now and at the hour of our death. *Amen.*

Hail, Mary, full of grace, the Lord is with thee.
Blessed art thou among women,
and blessed is the fruit of thy womb, Jesus.

Holy Mary, Mother of God, pray for us sinners,
now and at the hour of our death. *Amen.*

Hail, Mary, full of grace, the Lord is with thee.
Blessed art thou among women,
and blessed is the fruit of thy womb, Jesus.

Holy Mary, Mother of God, pray for us sinners,
now and at the hour of our death. *Amen.*

Hail, Mary, full of grace, the Lord is with thee.
Blessed art thou among women,
and blessed is the fruit of thy womb, Jesus.

Holy Mary, Mother of God, pray for us sinners,
now and at the hour of our death. *Amen.*

Hail, Mary, full of grace, the Lord is with thee.
  Blessed art thou among women,
    and blessed is the fruit of thy womb, Jesus.

  Holy Mary, Mother of God, pray for us sinners,
    now and at the hour of our death. *Amen.*

Hail, Mary, full of grace, the Lord is with thee.
Blessed art thou among women,
and blessed is the fruit of thy womb, Jesus.

Holy Mary, Mother of God, pray for us sinners,
now and at the hour of our death. *Amen.*

Hail, Mary, full of grace, the Lord is with thee.
Blessed art thou among women,
and blessed is the fruit of thy womb, Jesus.

Holy Mary, Mother of God, pray for us sinners,
now and at the hour of our death. *Amen.*

Glory be to the Father,
and to the Son, and to the Holy Spirit;
as it was in the beginning, is now,
and ever shall be, world without end.
Amen.

O my Jesus, forgive us our sins,
save us from the fires of hell;
lead all souls to heaven, especially
those in most need of thy mercy.

The Coronation

A great sign appeared in the sky:
a woman clothed with the sun,
with the moon under her feet,
and on her head,
a crown of twelve stars.

The woman is Mary,
the one God chose
as the first to be purified
by the blood of the cross;
the one who said yes
to God's Word,
and the one in whom
the Word became flesh;
the one who carried Jesus
in her womb, and in her arms,
and in her heart;
the one Jesus gave to us,
saying, "Behold, your mother."

INTENTIONS

Our Father
  who art in heaven,
  hallowed be thy name.
Thy kingdom come.
Thy will be done on earth,
  as it is in heaven.

Give us this day our daily bread,
and forgive us our trespasses,
as we forgive those
  who trespass against us,
and lead us not into temptation,
  but deliver us from evil.

Amen.

Hail, Mary, full of grace, the Lord is with thee.
Blessed art thou among women,
and blessed is the fruit of thy womb, Jesus.

Holy Mary, Mother of God, pray for us sinners,
now and at the hour of our death. *Amen.*

Hail, Mary, full of grace, the Lord is with thee.
   Blessed art thou among women,
      and blessed is the fruit of thy womb, Jesus.

Holy Mary, Mother of God, pray for us sinners,
   now and at the hour of our death.   *Amen.*

Hail, Mary, full of grace, the Lord is with thee.
Blessed art thou among women,
and blessed is the fruit of thy womb, Jesus.

Holy Mary, Mother of God, pray for us sinners,
now and at the hour of our death. *Amen.*

Hail, Mary, full of grace, the Lord is with thee.
  Blessed art thou among women,
     and blessed is the fruit of thy womb, Jesus.

Holy Mary, Mother of God, pray for us sinners,
  now and at the hour of our death. *Amen.*

Hail, Mary, full of grace, the Lord is with thee.
  Blessed art thou among women,
    and blessed is the fruit of thy womb, Jesus.

Holy Mary, Mother of God, pray for us sinners,
  now and at the hour of our death. *Amen.*

Hail, Mary, full of grace, the Lord is with thee.
Blessed art thou among women,
and blessed is the fruit of thy womb, Jesus.

Holy Mary, Mother of God, pray for us sinners,
now and at the hour of our death. *Amen.*

Hail, Mary, full of grace, the Lord is with thee.
Blessed art thou among women,
and blessed is the fruit of thy womb, Jesus.

Holy Mary, Mother of God, pray for us sinners,
now and at the hour of our death. *Amen.*

Hail, Mary, full of grace, the Lord is with thee.
Blessed art thou among women,
and blessed is the fruit of thy womb, Jesus.

Holy Mary, Mother of God, pray for us sinners,
now and at the hour of our death. *Amen.*

Hail, Mary, full of grace, the Lord is with thee.
Blessed art thou among women,
and blessed is the fruit of thy womb, Jesus.

Holy Mary, Mother of God, pray for us sinners,
now and at the hour of our death. *Amen.*

Hail, Mary, full of grace, the Lord is with thee.
Blessed art thou among women,
and blessed is the fruit of thy womb, Jesus.

Holy Mary, Mother of God, pray for us sinners,
now and at the hour of our death. *Amen.*

Glory be to the Father,
  and to the Son, and to the Holy Spirit;
as it was in the beginning, is now,
and ever shall be, world without end.
  Amen.

O my Jesus, forgive us our sins,
save us from the fires of hell;
lead all souls to heaven, especially
those in most need of thy mercy.

Hail, holy Queen,
Mother of Mercy:
our life, our sweetness and our hope.
To thee do we cry,
poor banished children of Eve;
To thee do we send up our sighs,
mourning and weeping in this valley of tears.
Turn then, most gracious advocate,
thine eyes of mercy toward us;
and after this our exile,
show unto us the blessed fruit of thy womb, Jesus.
O clement, O loving,
O sweet Virgin Mary.

V. Pray for us, O holy Mother of God.

R. That we may be made worthy of the
promises of Christ.

In the name of the Father, and of the Son,
and of the Holy Spirit. *Amen.*

Art Credits

Cover and title page: Annibale Carracci, *The Coronation of the Virgin*, after 1595.

Title page, 23, 39, 55, 71, 87, back cover: Jessica Connelly, *Glorious Mysteries Rose Wreath*, 2018. All rights reserved. Used with permission. Artist website: https://telos.design

2–3: Antwerp, *Madonna of the Rosary,* early 19th century. Licensed from Adobe Stock.

5: Andrei Rublev, *Holy Trinity*, 1425–1427.

7: Giulio Cesare Procaccini, *Madonna and Child with Saints Francis and Dominic and Angels*, c. 1612.

THE RESURRECTION

8–9: Lucas Cranach, *The Resurrected Christ in Limbo with Adam and Eve*, 1562. Licensed from Adobe Stock.

10–11: Peter Paul Rubens, *Christ Triumphing over Death and Sin*, 1615–1616. Photography by Rama. Licensed under CC BY-SA 2.0.

12: Sebastiano Ricci, *The Resurrection*, 1715–1716.

13: Pascal Dagnan-Bouveret, *Christ and the Disciples at Emmaus*, 1896–1897. Photography by Moira Burke. Licensed under CC BY-SA 2.0.

14: Master of the Amsterdam Death of the Virgin, *The Resurrection*, 1485–1500.

15: Peter Paul Rubens, Christ Risen, 1616. Image provided by Scala / Art Resource, NY.

16: Pieter Lastman, *The Resurrection*, 1612.

17: Jan Boeckhorst, panel from the Snyders Triptych, 1659.

18: Peter Paul Rubens, *Noli Me Tangere*, 17th century.

19: Alexander Andreyevich Ivanov, *Christ's Appearance to Mary Magdalene after the Resurrection*, 1835.

20–21: Guillam Forchondt and Willem van Herp, *Noli Me Tangere*, 1678.

22: Caravaggio, *The Incredulity of Saint Thomas*, 1601–1602.

THE ASCENSION

24–25: Benjamin West, *The Ascension*, 1801.

26–27: Gustave Doré, *The Ascension*, 1879.

28: Francesco Salviati, *The Ascension of the Lord*, 16th century. Licensed from Adobe Stock.

29: Johann Koerbecke, *The Ascension*, 1456.

30: Gebhard Fugel, *Ascension of Christ*, Fresken von Gebhard Fugel, 1894.

31: Unknown artist, painting in the chapel of the Mother's Village, Medjugorje. Licensed from Adobe Stock.

32: Bernardino Gandino, *Ascension of the Lord*, early 17th century. Licensed from Adobe Stock.

33: Rembrandt, *The Ascension*, 1636.

34: Guillaume Fouace, *The Ascension*, 1878.

35: John Singleton Copley, *The Ascension*, 1775.

36: Giacomo Cavedone, *Ascension of Christ*, 1640.

37: Unknown artist, Ascension of Christ stained glass. Licensed from Adobe Stock.

38: Francisco Camilo, *Ascension*, 1651.

DESCENT OF THE HOLY SPIRIT

40–41: Juan Bautista Mayno, *Pentecost*, 1612–1614.

42–43: Bardi Barth, Mysteries of the Rosary: *The Descent of the Holy Spirit*. Copyright © HERBRONNEN vzw. All rights reserved. Used with permission. Artist website: www.bradi-barth.org

44–45: Jean II Restout, *Pentecost*, 1732.

46: El Greco, *Pentecost*, 1596.

47: Master of the Dominican Effigies, *Pentecost*, 1340.

48: Gian Domenico Facchina, Pentecost mosaic in the Rosary Bailica, Lourdes, France, c. 1895–1907.

49: Daniel Bell, *Pentecost*, 1870s. Photo by Fr. Lawrence Lew, OP. Used with permission.

50: Unknown artist, detail from rosary altar in Friesach, Austria.

51: Pentecost mosaic in the Cathedral Basilica of St. Louis (Missouri). Photography: Pete Unseth. Licensed under CC BY-SA 4.0.

52: Michael Zulu, *Pentecost*. Faustino House of the Society of Mary. (Lusaka, Zambia). Photography by Erica Rudemiller. Used with permission.

53: Bohemian Master, *The Pentecost*, 1413–1415.

54: Franz Plattner, *Deckenbild*, 1876. Photography by Böhringer Friedrich. Licensed under CC BY-SA 2.5.

THE ASSUMPTION

56–57: Priest Victor, *The Dormition of the Virgin*, Second half of the 17th century.

58–59: Tim Langenderfer, *The Assumption*, 2010. All rights reserved. Used with permission. Artist website: timlangenderfer.com

60: Nicolas Poussin, *The Assumption of the Virgin*, 1630–1632.

61: Ruizanglada, *Assumption*, 1998. All rights reserved. Used with permission. Artist website: ruizanglada.es

62: Unknown artist, fresco of the Assumption in the Church of the Trinita Dei Monti (Rome, Italy). Licensed from Adobe Stock.

63: Nicola Filotesio, *Assumption of the Virgin*, 1515.

64: Juan Carreño de Miranda, *Assumption of the Virgin*, 1657.

65: Laurent de La Hyre, *The Assumption*, c. 1653–1655.

66: Painting of the Assumption in the Cerasi Chapel of the Basilica of Santa Maria del Popolo. Photography © José Luiz Bernardes Ribeiro / CC BY-SA 4.0.

67: Annibale Carracci, *Assumption of Mary*, 1590.

68: Guido Reni, *The Assumption of Virgin Mary*, 1639.

69: Frei Carlos, *Assumption of the Virgin*, 1520's. Photography by Rick Morais. Licensed under CC BY-SA 4.0.

70: Paolo di Giovanni Fei, *The Assumption of the Virgin with Busts of the Archangel Gabriel and the Virgin of the Annunciation*, 1400–1405.

THE CORONATION

72–73: Sandro Botticelli, *Madonna and Child*, 1480–1481.

74–75: Diego Velázquez, *Coronation of the Virgin*, 1635–1636.

76: Gentile da Fabriano, *The Coronation of the Virgin*, 1422–1425.

77: Agnolo Gaddi, *The Coronation of the Virgin*, 1380–1385.

78: Franz Ittenbach, *Madonna and Child*, c. 1862.

79: Michel Sittow, *The Assumption of the Virgin*, 1500.

80: Annibale Carracci, *The Coronation of the Virgin*, 1595.

81: Oddone Pascale, *Coronation of Mary*, 16th century. Licensed from Adobe Stock.

82: Fra Angelico, *The Coronation of the Virgin*, 1430–1435.

83: Unknown artist, Mary Help of Christians in the Basilica of Mary Help of Christians, Turin, Italy. Licensed from Adobe Stock.

84: Fra Angelico, *The Coronation of the Virgin*, 1434–1435.

85: William–Adolphe Bouguereau, *The Queen of the Angels*, 1900.

86: Tara Vanessa Hall, *Mary Queen of Heaven*. All rights reserved. Used with permission. Artist website: etsy.com/shop/PerfectJoyPaintings

88: Unknown. Licensed from Adobe Stock.

Back cover: Peter Paul Rubens, *Christ Triumphing over Death and Sin*, 1615–1616. Photography by Rama. Licensed under CC BY-SA 2.0.

How to Pray the Rosary with This Book

WELCOME to THE ILLUMINATED ROSARY, a way of praying the rosary more meditatively with the help of sacred art. THE ILLUMINATED ROSARY was first developed for families with young children, but has proven popular with young and old alike.

Using THE ILLUMINATED ROSARY is simple:

- The *full text* of every prayer is printed in order, so that young readers might learn to pray the rosary without distraction.

- Each mystery is introduced with a brief, *child-friendly reading* loosely based on the Scriptures. In the rosary, a mystery is an episode in the life of Christ or Mary that unfolds God's plan of salvation. After reading about each mystery, you will be prompted to state the *intentions* for which you are praying.

- The *sacred art* on every spread is meant to aid prayerful meditation. As you pray each decade, remember the words of Pope Paul VI: "By its nature the recitation of the Rosary calls for a quiet rhythm and a lingering pace, helping the individual to meditate on the mysteries of the Lord's life..." (Pope Paul VI, Marialis Cultus #47).

- The roses around the text of each Hail Mary serve as *rosary beads*, helping kids keep track of where they are in the decade.

Here are some practical suggestions for praying THE ILLUMINATED ROSARY with children:

- *Keep it short* at first, saying one decade of the rosary in a single sitting. *Try praying antiphonally*: one group or person says the first half of each prayer, and the other group or person says the second half.

- Optionally, *ask your family for intentions* for each decade. For whom or for what do you wish to offer the prayers of the decade?

- After you are finished praying, *ask your children what thoughts or feelings* they had as they meditated on each mystery. Which artwork "spoke" to them most? How might the Holy Spirit have been speaking to them through their meditation?

You may find some of the artwork in these pages not to your personal taste. That is natural; but to get the most out of your meditation, try viewing these images sympathetically. Let the vision of the artist challenge you: Why would the artist paint the mystery as he or she did? What does it reveal to the artist and others who have appreciated it? However you use THE ILLUMINATED ROSARY, may praying with it lead you closer to the heart of Jesus through the heart of his mother; and may your own heart be filled with awe, reverence, and wonder.

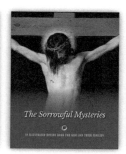

The Joyful Mysteries

The Luminous Mysteries

The Sorrowful Mysteries

The Glorious Mysteries

Dedicated to the memory of Norman G. Daoust.

Nihil obstat:
Rev. Timothy Hall, *Censor librorum*

Imprimatur:
†Most Rev. John M. Quinn, Bishop of Winona
May 13, 2015

The imprimatur is an official declaration that a book or pamphlet is free of doctrinal or moral error. No implication is contained therein that those who have granted the imprimatur agree with the contents, opinions, or statements expressed.

The Illuminated Rosary, Revised Edition
The Glorious Mysteries
An Illustrated Rosary Book for Kids and Their Families

24 23 22 21 20 19   2 3 4 5 6 7 8 9

ISBN: 978-1-68192-513-4 (Inventory No. T2402)
LCCN: 2019939989

Book design and build by Steve Nagel.
Acknowledgments assistance by Sara Dethloff.
Proofing by Karen Carter.

See art credits, page 90, for copyright statements pertaining to individual artworks.

Our Sunday Visitor Publishing
www.osv.com